ART ATTACK

with Neil Buchanan

DORLING KINDERSLEY
London • New York • Moscow • Sydney

A Dorling Kindersley Book

Art Editor Cheryl Telfer
Additional Design Vanessa Hamilton
Editor Lee Simmons
Senior Editor Sue Peach

Prop Maker Jim Copley
Photographer Gary Ombler

Senior Art Editor Marcus James
Managing Editor Jane Yorke
Production Charlotte Traill
DTP Designer Almudena Díaz

Published in Great Britain by
Dorling Kindersley Limited
9 Henrietta Street, London WC2E 8PS
2 4 6 8 10 9 7 5 3

A CIP catalogue record for this book
is available from the British Library.

ISBN: 0-7513-5626-3

Colour reproduction by GRB Editrice S.r.l., Verona, Italy
Printed and bound in Italy by L.E.G.O.

Dorling Kindersley would like to thank everyone at Media Merchants
for their help and enthusiasm.

Additional thanks to Mark Haygarth for jacket design and
Andy Crawford for additional photography.

CONTENTS

INTRODUCTION

Hi and welcome to the Art Attack book – which is packed with rubbish, or to be more accurate, it's packed with fantastic Art Attacks that you can make using everyday things that you can find around your home. Have a go! Try making these yourself – and give yourself an Art Attack. Remember you don't have to be good at art to be a GREAT artist. Good luck and have fun!

Neil Buchanan

Crêpe paper

Party cups

Cardboard tubes

Dry pasta

Wrapping paper

String

Wire

Kitchen paper

Paintbrushes

Marker pens ★

Glue mixture
You will need to make this special glue mixture for many of the projects in the book. Use twice as much PVA glue as water to make a really strong mixture.

Two parts PVA glue

One part water

Finished glue mixture

★ *Make sure you open nearby windows before using marker pens.*

Tape

Cardboard

Balloons

Glitter

Hints and tips
Look out for
The Head on the
pages of this book. He
appears throughout,
giving you advice,
hints, and tips for
your projects.

Corrugated
cardboard

Coloured
pencils

Toilet
paper

Coloured
card

Gold and silver
marker pens

Plastic bag

Cotton wool

Poster
paint

Acrylic
paints

Newspaper

Art Attack bin
Keep a watch on the
rubbish your family
throws away – that
discarded newspaper,
box, or packet might
be just what you need!

HORROR HANGER

A re you tired of people tidying up your wardrobe
or borrowing your clothes without permission?
If so, scare them off with a horror hanger.

From cardboard to monster

Materials

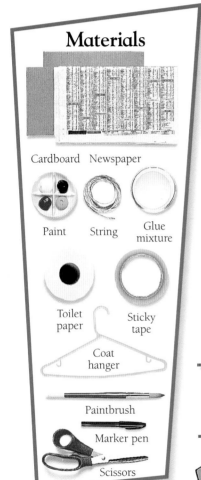

Cardboard   Newspaper

Paint   String   Glue mixture

Toilet paper   Sticky tape

Coat hanger

Paintbrush

Marker pen

Scissors

1 Draw a life-size horror head on to some cardboard. Make sure the neck is as long as the head and then cut it out.

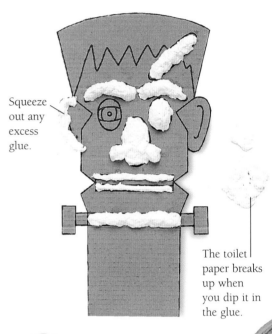

Squeeze out any excess glue.

The toilet paper breaks up when you dip it in the glue.

2 Dip toilet paper into the glue mixture and use it to build up features on the face.

When the toilet paper and glue dries, the card will be very firm.

3 Cover the front and back of the horror head with a layer of toilet paper. Paint the whole head with the glue mixture and leave it to dry.

Highlight facial features with paint.

4 Finish off the horror head by painting it in bright colours. Make your head look as horrible and scary as possible.

Frightful Frankenstein

When fully dressed, your horror hanger will give wardrobe intruders a fright!

Kitchen foil will make the neck bolt look metallic.

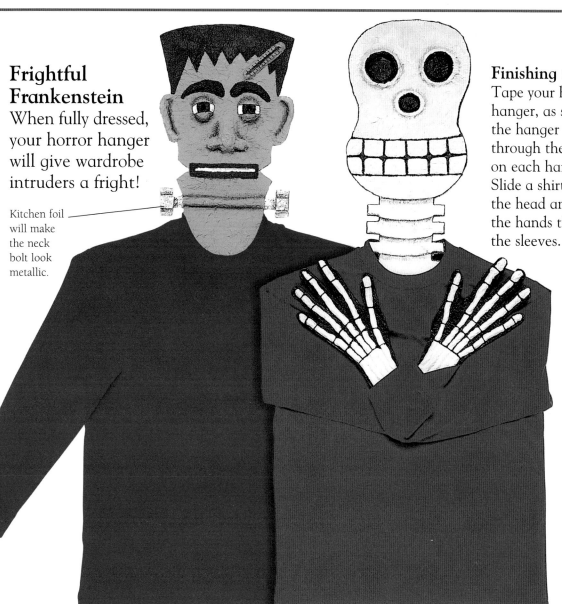

Finishing touches

Tape your horror head to a coat hanger, as shown. Tie strings to the hanger and through the hole on each hand. Slide a shirt over the head and slip the hands through the sleeves.

Hook your hanger to string tied along your clothes rail.

Thread string through the holes in the hands.

Spooky skeleton

Try making more scary horror hangers, like this spooky skeleton painted white and black.

Making the horror hands

1 Trace around your hands on a piece of cardboard. Cut out the shapes with a pair of scissors.

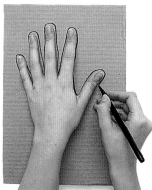

Carefully pierce a hole in the bottom of each hand.

Paint the paper strips white and black to look like bony fingers.

2 Lay long, twisted strips of newspaper along each finger, and tape or glue them down. Leave them to dry.

3 Cover both sides of the hands with one layer of toilet paper and glue mixture. Leave to dry, then paint them the same colour as your horror head.

BEASTLY BANK

W ho needs a boring piggy bank when you can make a dinosaur bank to guard your pocket money? Just drop coins in the slot and start saving!

From balloon to bank

Materials

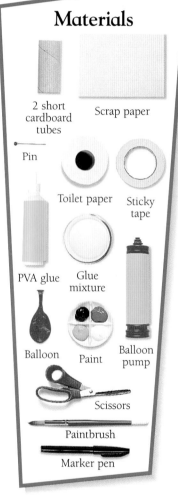

2 short cardboard tubes

Scrap paper

Pin

Toilet paper

Sticky tape

PVA glue

Glue mixture

Balloon

Paint

Balloon pump

Scissors

Paintbrush

Marker pen

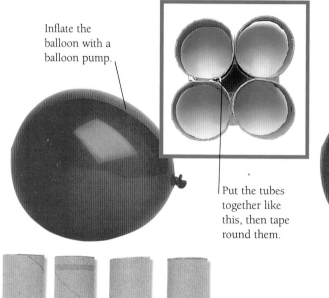

Inflate the balloon with a balloon pump.

Put the tubes together like this, then tape round them.

This rectangle will become the money slot.

1 Blow up a small, round balloon and then tie the end. Cut two cardboard tubes in half and tape the four pieces together.

2 Tape the balloon on top of the cardboard tube legs. Use a marker pen to draw a small rectangle (about 1 cm x 4 cm) on top of the balloon.

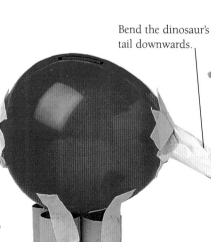

Use scrap paper that is roughly the same length as the balloon.

Bend the dinosaur's tail downwards.

3 Crunch up a piece of paper and bend it slightly upwards. Tape the paper to the front of the balloon to make the dinosaur's neck. Do the same with a second piece of paper and tape it to the back of the balloon to make the tail.

Use a lighter shade of paint on the dinosaur's underside.

Do not cover
the money slot.

Glue two small
balls of paper on to
the head for eyes.

4 Wrap toilet paper around the body, neck, and tail, then brush on the glue mixture. Cover the dinosaur with three or four layers of paper and glue mixture, then leave it overnight to dry.

5 Paint the dinosaur when it is hard and dry. Once the paint has dried, cover the dinosaur with a layer of PVA glue to give it a shiny finish. Then stick a pin through the money slot to pop the balloon.

Artattackasaurus

Your dinosaur bank can be any colour you like. An Artattackasaurus can even have spots and scales!

This short, stumpy tail is made from a thick wad of paper.

These scales are made from triangles of card.

Paint the eyes white with black pupils in the middle.

Paint the teeth and claws in white, then outline them in black pen.

Spending money
Stick a blunt knife into the slot and turn the bank upside down. Coins will slide out down the knife.

9

ANCIENT MASK

Y ou don't need to dig up old ruins to find an ancient mask. Just start with a cardboard box and create some home-made history!

Materials

Cardboard box

Paper   Paint

Tissue paper

Scissors   Sticky tape

Glue mixture   Toilet paper

Paintbrush

Marker pen

From box to mask

Make sure the shield shape is at least 25 cm from top to bottom.

Start drawing from the paper fold.

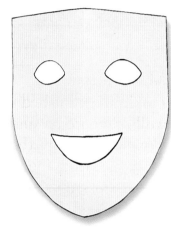

1 Fold a piece of paper in half. With the folded edge on the left, draw half a shield shape, half a mouth, and one eye.

2 Carefully cut out the mouth and eye, then cut around the shield. Open up the paper and you have a mask template.

Draw a line joining the top two corners to form the top of the mask.

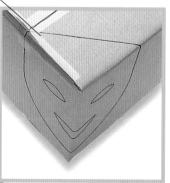

Twist toilet paper into curly shapes and stick them down with glue.

Decorate around the eyes and mouth with toilet paper.

3 Tape the mask template on to the corner of a cardboard box. Trace around the mask, remembering to include the eyes and mouth.

4 Remove the template, then cut out the mask, eyes, and mouth. Fold a piece of paper into a basic nose shape, and tape it in place. Make eyebrows the same way.

5 Place small strips of coloured tissue paper on to the mask, then brush the glue mixture on top. Cover both sides of the mask, making sure you get inside all the corners.

6 Leave the mask to dry overnight. Use a ball of toilet paper to dab yellow or metallic paint over the mask, but don't press the paint into the creases. Then leave the paint to dry.

Mask museum

Display the finished mask on a wall to create an ancient effect. Try making more than one mask and turn your bedroom into a mask museum!

Hang the back of the mask over a nail or hook.

Decorate with black tissue paper and silver paint.

Vicious Viking

To create a Viking mask, draw a paper template with a sharp, pointed chin. Add scrunched-up newspaper to make a helmet.

The metallic paint creates a cracked, ancient effect.

The smiling mouth gives this mask a friendly expression.

FANTASY CASTLE

Have you ever dreamed about having your very own castle, just like in a fairytale? Why not build one from cardboard tubes? It's easy!

Materials

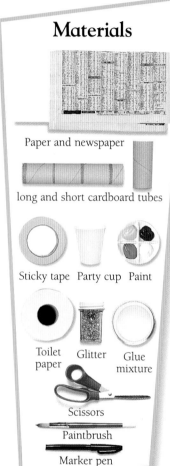

Paper and newspaper

long and short cardboard tubes

Sticky tape   Party cup   Paint

Toilet paper   Glitter   Glue mixture

Scissors

Paintbrush

Marker pen

From tubes to castle

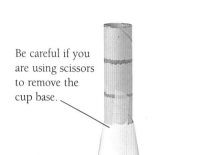

Be careful if you are using scissors to remove the cup base.

1 Tape a party cup upside down on a piece of paper. Cut or tear off the base of the cup and stick a long cardboard tube inside. Tape it in place.

Tape the newspaper in place.

Block the tubes with balls of scrunched up newspaper.

2 Tape two long cardboard tubes to the cup, one on each side. Tape a third long tube behind the middle tube and slightly higher.

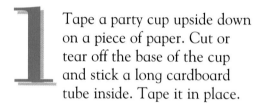

Each window is an arch shape with a straight base.

5 Cover each of the short tubes with a paper cone. Carefully tape the cones in place. These cones will be the turret roofs. Don't worry about the pieces of tape looking untidy as they will get covered with paper later.

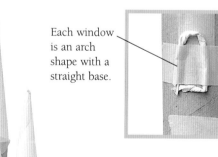

6 Next, take some short strips of paper and twist them tightly to make them long and thin. Bend these into curved shapes to make arches, then tape them to the fantasy castle to make windows and a door.

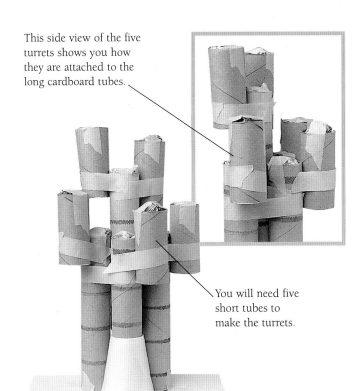

This side view of the five turrets shows you how they are attached to the long cardboard tubes.

You will need five short tubes to make the turrets.

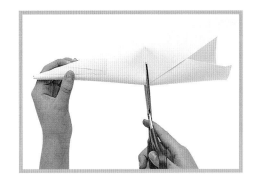

Cut the cone so it is roughly the same height as the short cardboard tubes and wide enough at the bottom to just fit over the tube end.

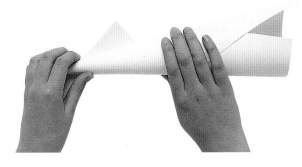

3 Tape a short cardboard tube to one side of the middle tube. Attach a short tube to each of the two side tubes. Finally, tape two short tubes to the sides of the rear tube, as shown above.

4 Start rolling up a piece of paper in one corner. As you roll, turn the paper to the right to form a cone. Tape along the edge of the paper to hold the cone in place. You will need to make a number of cones.

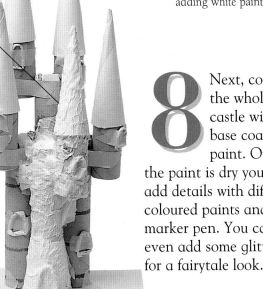

When it dries, the toilet paper strengthens the castle and gives it a stone effect.

You can create lighter shades of a colour by adding white paint.

7 Place strips of toilet paper over the cardboard tubes and brush with the glue mixture. Cover the whole of the castle, including the base, with three layers of toilet paper and glue mixture. Then leave until it is completely dry.

8 Next, cover the whole castle with a base coat of paint. Once the paint is dry you can add details with different coloured paints and a marker pen. You can even add some glitter for a fairytale look.

DREAM CASTLE

This is the castle of your dreams, so decorate it any way you like. Here are a few ideas, but there is no limit to the magnificent mansions that you can create.

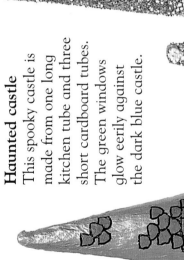

Darker blue stones outlined in black add texture to the castle.

Draw black window bars on the white windows.

Paint the turrets yellow or gold and add glitter for a fairytale look.

Haunted castle
This spooky castle is made from one long kitchen tube and three short cardboard tubes. The green windows glow eerily against the dark blue castle.

Paint tiles on the roof and stones around the window frames for realistic detail.

Draw on other castle features for a fortress effect.

Fairytale fortress

Who would you invite to live in your fantasy fortress? A moat, a drawbridge, and silver bars on the door keep unwanted visitors away from this dream palace.

Paint a path of grey cobblestones leading to a dark, foreboding door with metallic hinges.

To add glitter, lay the castle on its side. Paint with PVA glue then sprinkle with glitter while the glue is still wet.

Saving your glitter

Lay the castle on a large sheet of paper to catch any glitter that falls off. Then roll up the paper and tip the glitter back into the jar.

A moat has been painted around the bottom of this castle.

SNAKE HOOK

Is your bedroom so full of clutter that you can never find anywhere to hang your clothes or your bags? What you need is a snake hook!

From cardboard to snake

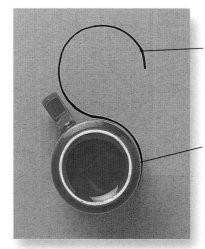

Starting on the right, draw three-quarters of the way round the mug.

Move the mug down to the bottom of your line and draw the other way round it.

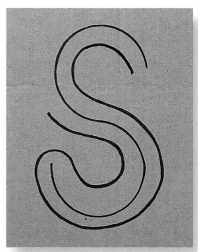

1 Place the corrugated cardboard so that the lines run top to bottom. Draw round the mug as shown above to make an S shape.

2 Fatten the S up by drawing a snake all round it, using the S line as the middle of your snake. The snake needs to be about 3 cm wide.

To make the head, fold one end of the newspaper back on its self and tape down.

Tape a paper ball to each side of the snake's head for the eyes.

3 Cut the snake out. Next, scrunch up a sheet of newspaper lengthways. Starting at the tail end, tuck and scrunch the paper along your snake, taping it securely into position as you go along.

4 Tape a second piece of scrunched up newspaper to the other side of your snake. Then roll up two small balls of newspaper to make the snake's eyes and tape them to its head.

5

Wrap strips of kitchen paper round your snake, then paint it with the glue mixture. Cover the whole snake with three layers of kitchen paper and glue mixture, so that the newspaper is completely covered.

6

Leave the snake to dry overnight, then draw on its eyes, mouth, nose, and some skin markings with a marker pen. Now you are ready to paint your snake in bright colours.

Balancing snake

You can hang your finished snake hook anywhere you like – in a wardrobe, on the back of a door, or what about on a shelf? Use it to hang up your clothes, your bags, or even your trainers.

Make it strong
You must use the cardboard with the corrugations running from top to bottom, as this gives your snake hook strength. Turn the cardboard round until a side with a wavy edge is at the top.

Hooded eyes and fearsome fangs make this snake look really mean!

Paint patterns of zig-zags, stripes, spots, or diamonds.

Paint the eyes and the fangs white.

Sleepy serpent
Here is an alternative snake, with a really sleepy look! Or how about making a giant snake by drawing round a dinner plate instead of a mug?

TROUSER BOWL

S tuck for an idea for an unusual present, or for somewhere to store bits and pieces? Why not make one of these funny trouser bowls?

From balloon to bowl

Cover the top part of the balloon with glue and paper.

You can use a plant pot or vase to hold the balloon in place as you work.

Use alternate layers of newspaper and magazine pages to show how many layers you have done.

Materials

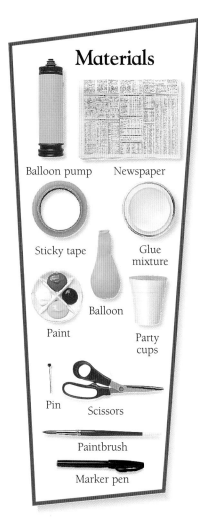

Balloon pump   Newspaper

Sticky tape   Glue mixture

Balloon

Paint   Party cups

Pin   Scissors

Paintbrush

Marker pen

1 Blow up the balloon with the pump. Paint the balloon with glue mixture, then cover it in small pieces of newspaper.

2 Cover the top two-thirds of the balloon with four layers of paper and glue mixture and leave to dry.

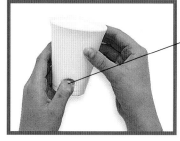

If you are using polystyrene cup, push a thumb through the side, near the base and rip the bottom off.

Ask someone to hold the bowl in place while you tape it.

3 When the bowl is completely dry, pop the balloon with a pin. Trim the rough edges of the bowl with scissors. Next, cut or tear the bottoms off two party cups.

4 Turn the two cups upside down and place them side by side. Put the bowl on top of the cups and tape them firmly in position so that they look like legs.

Bowls on legs

You can display just about anything in your trouser bowl. You could fill it with dried flowers, keep wrapped sweets in it, or even use it to store your art equipment.

Use a gold or silver marker pen to colour the buckle.

Blue jeans
A blue colour makes the trousers look like jeans. Add a brown belt, then draw the pockets, rivets, and stitching with fine marker pens.

Paint the inside of the bowl as well as the outside.

Paint on a patch and the stitching round it.

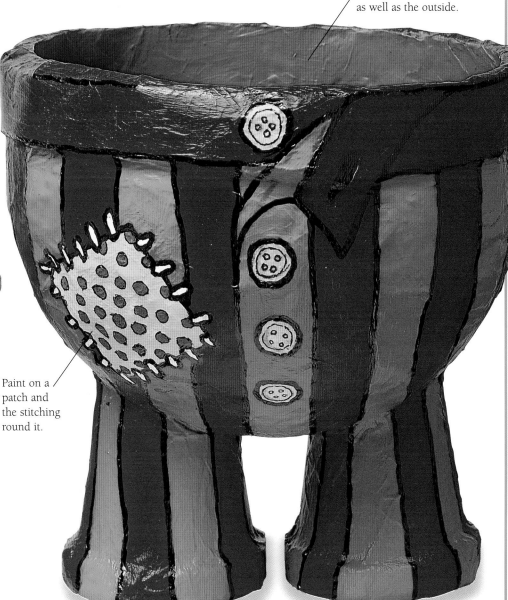

5 Cover the cups in four layers of glue and newspaper. Add thin, extra layers round the top of the bowl and the bottom of the two cups to make the waistband and turn-ups.

6 Leave the trousers to dry overnight, then paint. Do the stripes first, then leave the paint to dry before adding details with a marker pen. You can cover it with PVA glue for a shiny finish.

PASTA FRAME

Here's an idea for making someone a very special present that will remind them of you – a picture of yourself in a pasta frame!

From pasta to frame

Materials

Cardboard and coloured paper

Pasta shapes   Paint   Glue stick

PVA glue   Photograph

Scissors

Ruler

Paintbrush

Marker pen

Pencil

Mark the position of your frame lines with a series of dots.

1 Cut a piece of coloured paper at least 3 cm larger all round than your photograph. Glue the photograph in the centre of it. Next, place the paper on to some corrugated cardboard and draw round it with a pencil.

2 Use the marker pen to draw a line 2 cm in from the pencil line, along all four sides. Next, use the width of your pasta shapes to mark another rectangle around the outside of the pencil line.

Inside edge of frame   Outside edge of frame

Don't worry about glue showing between the pasta.

3 The rectangles drawn on the cardboard in marker pen form the inside and outside edges of your frame. Carefully cut out the frame, cutting around the outer rectangle first.

4 Cover the front of the frame in a thick layer of PVA glue. Then, arrange the pasta shapes in an attractive pattern on the frame, pressing them into the glue. Leave your frame to dry overnight.

Decorative frames

You can make pasta frame gifts to suit everyone. There are loads of different pasta shapes to use, and you can paint them any colour you like. Try gold or silver paint like the frames shown here, to add a touch of luxury.

Different pasta shapes can be arranged in an alternating pattern.

You've been framed!

Your frame doesn't have to be rectangular. You can make square ones, oval ones – any shape you like! The circular frame shown here is just right for a close-up of someone's face.

You can frame any picture you like. It can be a photograph, a painting you have done, or even a picture from a magazine.

Choose some colourful paper to make your border.

The glue will dry to a shiny finish.

5 Now, paint your frame, making sure you get the paint into all the corners. Leave the paint to dry, then cover the frame in a layer of PVA glue and let that dry, too.

Make sure your photograph is in the centre of your frame.

6 Put a thin line of glue along the outer edge of the coloured border. Then, carefully press your frame down on to it. Leave the finished frame to dry.

PICTURE MOBILE

O nce you've made this very simple, but effective mobile, you'll want to make lots more!

From cardboard to mobile

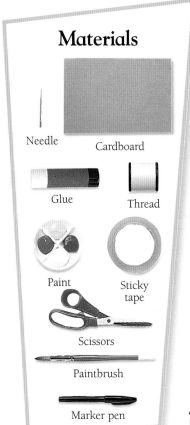

Materials

Needle

Cardboard

Glue

Thread

Paint

Sticky tape

Scissors

Paintbrush

Marker pen

Adding the smaller shapes gives the shapes a 3-D effect.

Cut out two circles for the Sun's centre.

1 Try drawing a Sun, rainbow, balloon, and two clouds as outline shapes on a piece of thick cardboard. Cut out the shapes as shown here.

2 Draw these shapes again, but this time make them smaller and do two of each shape. Cut them out and glue one to each side of the bigger pieces.

Paint the clouds in shades of white and grey.

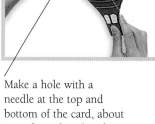

Make a hole with a needle at the top and bottom of the card, about 1 cm from the edge, for the thread to go through.

3 When the glue has dried, paint the cardboard shapes in bold colours. Don't forget to paint both sides of each shape.

4 Tie a length of thread through the hole at the bottom of each piece. Decide the order you want them to hang in, then tie them together, 5 cm apart.

Weather mobile

Now it's just a case of choosing where to hang up your finished mobile!

A smiling face on the Sun makes the mobile look fun.

Add a loop to the top so you can hang up your mobile.

Stick on some big cardboard eyes to make your octopus come alive!

Emphasize the shapes by drawing outlines in black.

Add in as many different shapes as you like.

Cut out green land shapes to stick on the blue Earth.

Paint spaces white instead of cutting them out.

Use dark-coloured paints to create shadows under the cloud.

Underwater creatures

You can pick any theme you like for your mobile. These sea creatures would look great in the bathroom!

Space adventure

If you're interested in the stars, why not design your own space mobile – complete with a friendly alien!

23

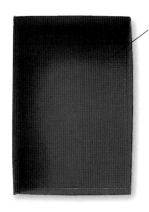

SHRUNKEN HEAD

Here's a piece of mad art, just for fun – a shrunken head in a decorated frame!

From balloon to head

Materials

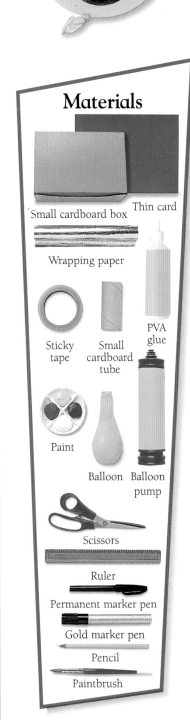

Small cardboard box   Thin card

Wrapping paper

Sticky tape   Small cardboard tube   PVA glue

Paint   Balloon   Balloon pump

Scissors

Ruler

Permanent marker pen

Gold marker pen

Pencil

Paintbrush

A tea-bag box or sweet box is an ideal size for your box.

Use the wrapping paper to line the back of the box.

1 Find a small cardboard box, such as a food package, and cut off the front. Paint the whole box, inside and out, using poster or acrylic paints.

2 Cut some fancy wrapping paper to the size of the back of the box. Spread glue over the back wall and stick the paper in.

Use a permanent marker pen to draw the face.

5 Cut out the middle rectangle and around the outside edge of the frame. Turn the frame over and decorate it using a gold marker pen or felt-tip pen.

6 Blow up a balloon, using a balloon pump, but do not tie it. Ask someone to hold the balloon while you draw a silly cartoon face on it.

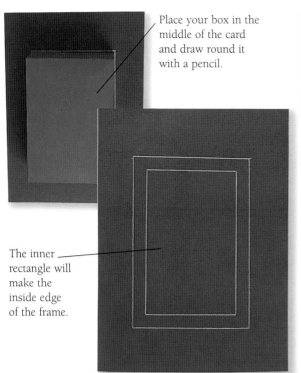

Place your box in the middle of the card and draw round it with a pencil.

The inner rectangle will make the inside edge of the frame.

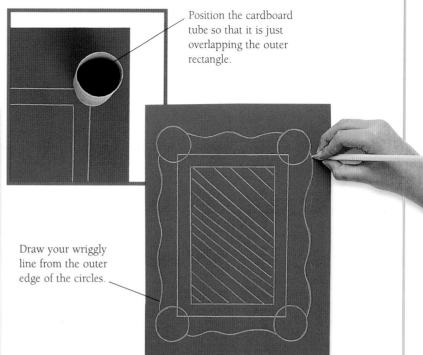

Position the cardboard tube so that it is just overlapping the outer rectangle.

Draw your wriggly line from the outer edge of the circles.

3 To make the frame, put your box on a piece of thin, brightly coloured card, and trace round it. Using a ruler, draw another rectangle, about 1 cm smaller, inside the box shape.

4 Place a cardboard tube in one corner of the frame and draw round it. Do this in each corner of the frame. Join up the four circles with a wriggly line to make the frame's outside edge.

Let the air out of the balloon slowly until it is about the same size as your fist. Then tie the balloon.

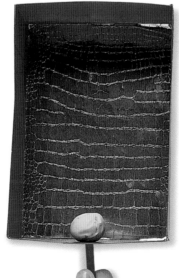

7 Let the balloon down so that it will fit in the box frame. Make a hole in the middle of the base of the box by pushing a pencil through it (see pages 62-63).

8 Pull the knot in the balloon through the hole in the bottom of the box frame. Your shrunken head should fit fairly snugly in the box.

SHOW OF HEADS

Here's a whole gallery of heads to give you some ideas. The heads get even funnier as they get older, because the balloons continue to shrink!

Laughing man

Stick the frame on your box, and it's finished – your very own shrunken head. Why not hang it on your bedroom wall and scare your friends!

Put the frame face down and position the cardboard box back on its original rectangle markings. Tape it in place.

Paint the teeth white and add white highlights to the eyes.

Permanent marker
You must use a permanent marker pen to draw the face on your balloon, otherwise the ink will smudge. Draw very carefully in case the balloon bursts!

Decorate the frame with fancy whirls and squirls.

A gold line and a row of dots gives a decorative edge.

Decorate the top of the frame with black marker pen.

Dracula on stage
Four pieces of card make this theatre's frame. The curtains are made of red card, and the stage top and bottom with gold card.

Strips of gold card.

Tape the two curtains to the box first. Then stick on the top and bottom of the stage.

Draw black lines on the curtains to show the folds in the fabric.

Balloon colours
Choose a balloon colour to suit your subject. Try making a cat from an orange balloon, or a Dalmatian dog from a white balloon decorated with black spots.

White highlights on the windows give the look of reflective glass.

Alien spacecraft
Cut a spaceship-shaped piece of card for this frame, then paint it with poster or acrylic paint. Draw the alien's face on a silver balloon with permanent marker and use acrylic paint for the nose.

This shrunken head hangs from the top of a square-shaped box.

27

FUNNY FACE

If you are holding a party and you want to liven it up, you need these wild party guests. Just hang them up and laugh at their funny faces!

From newspaper to weed

Materials

Newspaper

Crêpe paper

String

Paint

Stapler

Scissors

Paintbrush

Marker pen

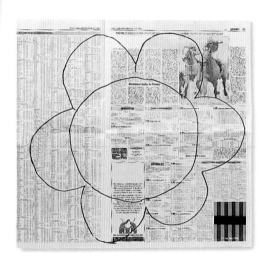

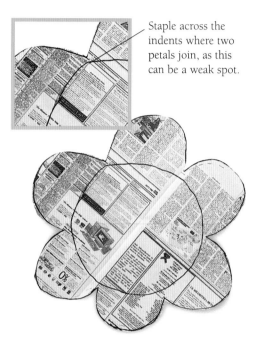

Staple across the indents where two petals join, as this can be a weak spot.

1 Lay two sheets of newspaper out flat and draw a flower shape with a marker pen. Hold the two sheets together and cut the shape out.

2 Holding the two flower shapes together, staple all round the edges. Leave a gap big enough to put your hand in.

Be careful not to rip the paper as you stuff your flower.

Paint the flower bright yellow with an orange centre.

3 Stuff your flower with strips of newspaper. Fill the petals first, but don't put too much stuffing in – the idea is to create a padded pillow shape. Then staple up the gap.

4 Now paint your flower. Acrylic paint is best for this because it gives a shiny flat finish, but you could also use poster paint.

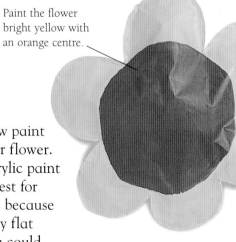

Add white highlights on the eyes and nose.

Outline all the features with a marker pen.

Stuff the face with newspaper, but leave the eyes flat.

Bed bug

Half-closed eyes and a lopsided grin give this bug its dopey expression. You could hang it up by your bed.

Friendly flower

When the paint is dry, decorate your flower by painting on a crazy face. Then, when it's party time, just hang it from the ceiling, a doorway, or a wall!

Tape a crêpe paper streamer to one of the lower petals to make the weed's stem.

To hang your flower, make a small hole between two petals, thread some string through, and knot it in place.

Manic monster

Leave a big gap for stuffing this monster as it has lots of awkward points to reach. Draw on bushy eyebrows, wild eyes, and ferocious fangs.

29

FRIDGE MAGNET

Are you always losing that important note or message? If so, then this unique fridge frame magnet is just what you need!

From cardboard to frame

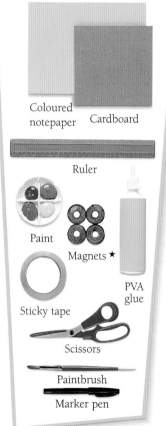

Materials

Coloured notepaper
Cardboard
Ruler
Paint
Magnets ★
PVA glue
Sticky tape
Scissors
Paintbrush
Marker pen

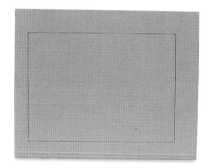

1 Take a sheet of the notepaper that you normally use and place it on a piece of thick cardboard. Hold the paper still with one hand and draw around its edge with a pencil.

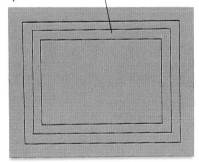

You will end up with three rectangles drawn on your piece of cardboard.

2 Measure 2 cm inside the rectangle you have drawn and draw another rectangle inside it. Then draw a third rectangle, 2 cm bigger than the first.

Cut out the hatched areas to make your frame.

3 The three rectangles you have drawn mark the frame's inside and outside edges and also the centre of the frame. Use them as guidelines and, with a marker pen, draw a lively border design.

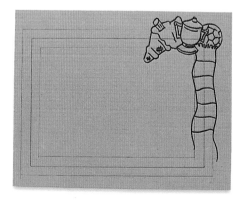

4 Your design can include things such as your favourite food or any hobbies or sports you enjoy. You can even include your name along the top. Whatever your design, it is very important that your design sticks out at least 2 cm either side of the central line.

★*Available from craft shops and hardware stores.*

Test your magnets before sticking them down.

5
When you're happy with your design, cut it out and colour it in with paint, felt-tip pens, or crayons. Pick out the details with a marker pen to give your frame a bold, cartoon-like effect.

6
When your design is complete, turn the frame over and glue a small fridge magnet to each of the four corners. Remember to test which side of the magnets will stick to your fridge door before you glue them in place.

Fridge reminder
Place your personalized fridge magnet frame over those important messages or pictures on your fridge and make them really stand out!

Make sure all parts of your design link together to make a continuous picture around the frame.

Take swimming things on Tuesday morning

Visit dentist
– Wednesday 4 o'clock

Toothy grin
This cartoon face frame with its toothy grin is just right for that important note about your visit to the dentist!

Magnet test
Test which side of the magnets will stick to the fridge. One side will stick – the other side will just slide off!

FACE BOWL

This cheeky character is actually a bowl! You can use it to keep anything you like in, and the lid will certainly keep the flies off.

From newspaper to bowl

Fold the cling wrap over the edges of the bowl.

Make the lid using the inside of one bowl.

Materials

Newspaper

Cling wrap

Bowls   Toilet paper

Glue mixture   Paint

Scissors

Paintbrush

Marker pen

1 Find two soup or breakfast bowls without rims to use as moulds for your bowl. Line the inside of one of the bowls with cling wrap.

2 Dip pieces of newspaper into the glue mixture. Press them on to the inside of the bowl, lining it with four or five layers of paper.

When it is dry, the bowl will lift out of the mould.

Make the base using the outside of the second bowl.

3 Turn the second bowl upside down, and cover the outside with cling wrap. Stick on layers of paper and glue as before. Let both bowls dry overnight.

4 When the bowls are dry, gently pull each one away from the cling wrap. Trim the top of each bowl with scissors to get a neat edge.

Cheeky chappie

Now paint the lid and base of your bowl with acrylic or poster paint. See what funny characters you can invent. Here are some ideas!

Add white highlights to the eyes.

You could use your bowl to keep wrapped sweets in.

Cross-eyed Charlie

Goofy teeth, round glasses, and cross eyes help to give this character a silly expression.

Use the nose as a handle to lift the lid on and off!

Remember to paint the inside of the bowl as well as the outside.

Place the nose in the centre of the lid.

Place two small balls on either side of the nose for nostrils.

5 Scrunch up some toilet paper and dip it into the glue. Squeeze out the excess glue. Shape the paper to make the nose and press it on to the lid. Leave it to dry.

6 With a marker pen, draw facial features on the lid. Don't try to draw a realistic face – make it as daft as you can! Draw ears and hair around the edge and then paint the lid.

3-D PICTURE

Everyone has ordinary, flat pictures on their walls, but why not go one better and make extra-ordinary 3-D pictures that really stand out!

From cardboard to frog

Materials

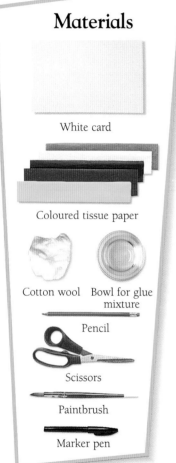

White card

Coloured tissue paper

Cotton wool   Bowl for glue mixture

Pencil

Scissors

Paintbrush

Marker pen

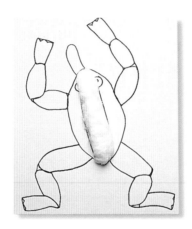

Tear off enough cotton wool to completely fill each section.

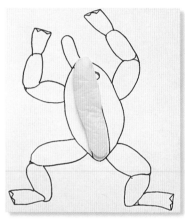

1 Draw a picture, like this frog, on some card and divide it into sections. Paint glue mixture on one of the sections then stick a ball of cotton wool to it.

2 Tear off some tissue paper big enough to cover the cotton wool section. Hold the tissue paper in place and carefully stick down the edges only.

Stick on two small balls of cotton wool wrapped in white tissue paper for the eyes.

Choose a bright red piece of tissue paper for your frog's tongue.

3 Build up the whole picture, section by section, colour by colour, in the same way. Tuck and glue the tissue paper in around the cotton wool as you go.

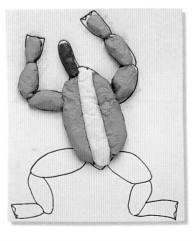

4 When your picture is finished, add in extra features such as the eyes, then leave it to dry overnight. Carefully cut the whole picture out, making sure you do not cut into the tissue paper.

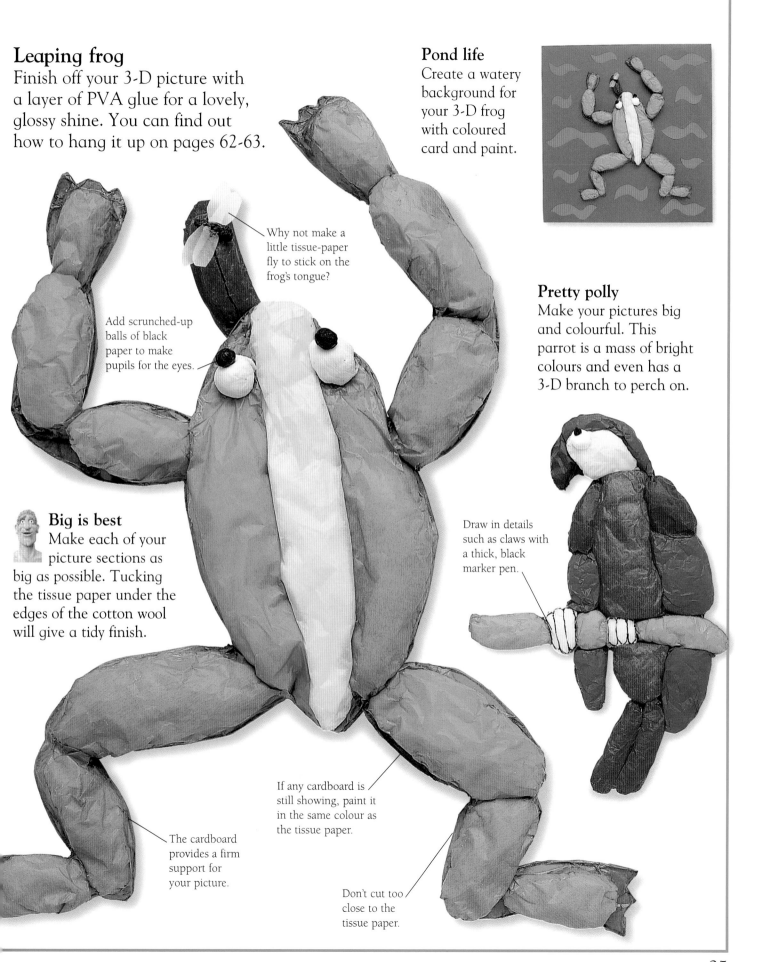

Leaping frog

Finish off your 3-D picture with
a layer of PVA glue for a lovely,
glossy shine. You can find out
how to hang it up on pages 62-63.

Pond life

Create a watery
background for
your 3-D frog
with coloured
card and paint.

Why not make a
little tissue-paper
fly to stick on the
frog's tongue?

Add scrunched-up
balls of black
paper to make
pupils for the eyes.

Pretty polly

Make your pictures big
and colourful. This
parrot is a mass of bright
colours and even has a
3-D branch to perch on.

Big is best

Make each of your
picture sections as
big as possible. Tucking
the tissue paper under the
edges of the cotton wool
will give a tidy finish.

Draw in details
such as claws with
a thick, black
marker pen.

The cardboard
provides a firm
support for
your picture.

If any cardboard is
still showing, paint it
in the same colour as
the tissue paper.

Don't cut too
close to the
tissue paper.

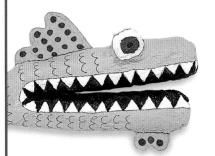

VICIOUS FISH

H ave you ever wanted a dangerous pet, but had nowhere to keep it? What you need is this vicious fish in its own tank.

From newspaper to fish

Materials

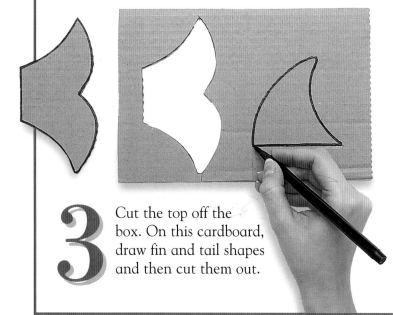

Cardboard box   Newspaper

Paint   Invisible thread   Glue mixture

Sticky tape   Toilet paper

Scissors

Paintbrush

Marker pen

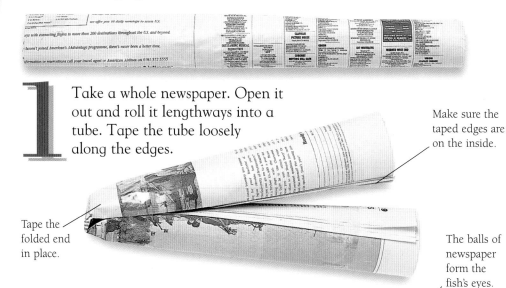

1 Take a whole newspaper. Open it out and roll it lengthways into a tube. Tape the tube loosely along the edges.

Tape the folded end in place.

Make sure the taped edges are on the inside.

The balls of newspaper form the fish's eyes.

2 Fold the paper tube in half so that one side is slightly longer than the other. Tape two balls of newspaper on to the top of the tube.

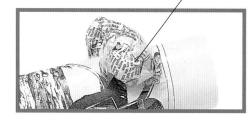

3 Cut the top off the box. On this cardboard, draw fin and tail shapes and then cut them out.

4 Stick the cardboard shapes on to the folded paper tube. Attach them securely with tape.

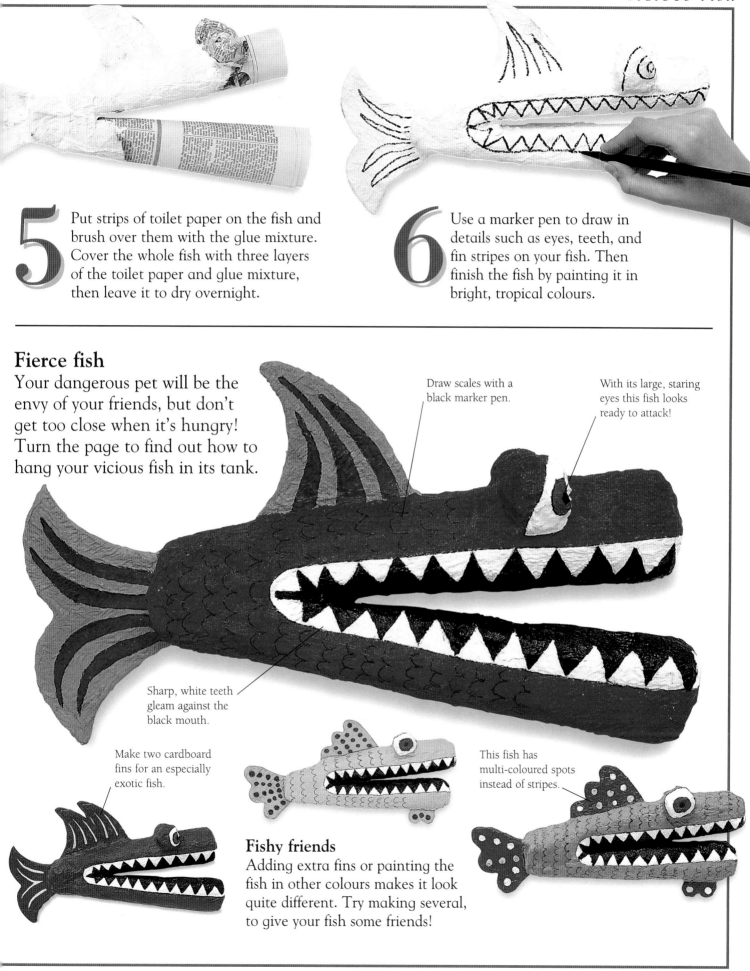

5 Put strips of toilet paper on the fish and brush over them with the glue mixture. Cover the whole fish with three layers of the toilet paper and glue mixture, then leave it to dry overnight.

6 Use a marker pen to draw in details such as eyes, teeth, and fin stripes on your fish. Then finish the fish by painting it in bright, tropical colours.

Fierce fish

Your dangerous pet will be the envy of your friends, but don't get too close when it's hungry! Turn the page to find out how to hang your vicious fish in its tank.

Draw scales with a black marker pen.

With its large, staring eyes this fish looks ready to attack!

Sharp, white teeth gleam against the black mouth.

Make two cardboard fins for an especially exotic fish.

This fish has multi-coloured spots instead of stripes.

Fishy friends

Adding extra fins or painting the fish in other colours makes it look quite different. Try making several, to give your fish some friends!

CRAZY FISH TANK

Once you've made your vicious fish, you'll need to put it in water. This crazy fish tank can hold one fish, or a whole shoal of them!

Making the tank

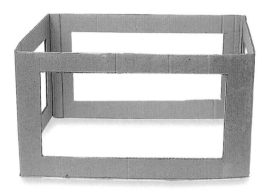

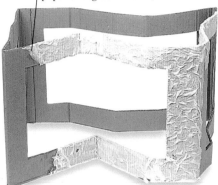

Cover the inside of the frame with paper and glue mixture, as well.

1 Cut the top and bottom out of the cardboard box. Then draw a large rectangle on each side of the box. Cut out the four rectangles to make the tank frame, as shown.

2 Crumple up the sides of the frame to give it a wavy shape. Then cover the frame with strips of toilet paper and glue mixture. Leave the frame to dry.

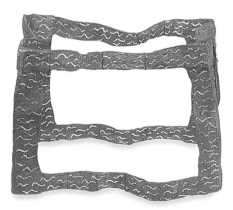

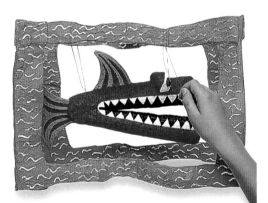

3 When the glue has dried, the frame will be solid. Paint your frame blue, then add small squiggly lines in white or silver paint to give the impression of watery ripples around your fish.

4 Wrap string or thread around the fish's mouth and tail and tie the ends to the top of the water tank. Transparent nylon thread, or fishing line, is good for this because it is almost invisible.

Finished tank

Make sure you give your finished tank pride of place on your shelf. Give the fish a gentle push and watch it swim from side to side.

A trio of terrors
This aquarium is home to three smaller fish. Hang them at different levels to fill your tank with snapping sharks!

Painting tips
Acrylic paints give a smooth finish. Mix them with water to make them spread easily, and don't forget that you can mix several colours together to create new shades.

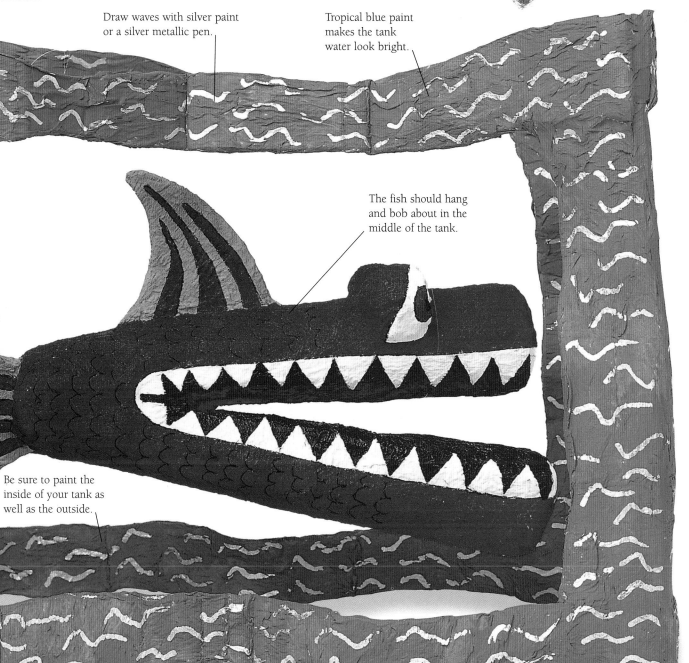

Draw waves with silver paint or a silver metallic pen.

Tropical blue paint makes the tank water look bright.

The fish should hang and bob about in the middle of the tank.

Be sure to paint the inside of your tank as well as the outside.

GIANT PENCIL

A re you for ever losing your pens and pencils? Here's a giant Art Attack pencil you'll never be able to mislay!

Materials

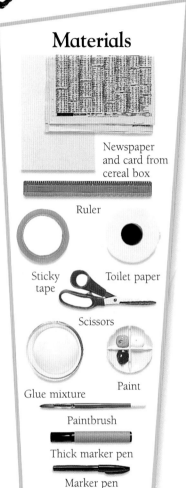

Newspaper and card from cereal box

Ruler

Sticky tape

Toilet paper

Scissors

Glue mixture

Paint

Paintbrush

Thick marker pen

Marker pen

From card to pencil

Use a ruler to divide the card into six equal strips.

Keep this end of the cone open and wide.

1 Cut the front off a cereal box and divide it lengthways into six equal strips. Fold the card along the lines. Overlap the two end strips and tape them firmly in position.

2 Divide the back of the box into quarters and cut one out. Make the pencil tip by folding over one corner of the card and rolling it up to form a cone shape, as shown.

Keep snipping small bits off the cone tip until the pen fits snugly inside.

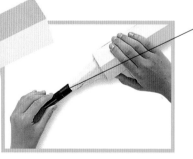

3 Stick the cone inside one end of the pencil body and tape it in position. You must tape it very securely, otherwise the pencil will fall apart when you try to write with it.

4 Snip off the tip of the cone and slip the thick marker pen inside. Tape the pen in position with just 1 cm of the pen and its lid sticking out of the cone.

The newspaper stuffing helps to make your pencil strong.

Be careful not to cover the tip, otherwise the pencil won't write.

Smooth the layers of paper down as you wrap them round the pencil.

5 Scrunch some pieces of newspaper into balls and stuff them into the pencil body. Use a ruler to press the paper right down into the tip. Tape across the open end to keep the stuffing in.

6 Paste glue mixture on to the sides of your pencil and then lay strips of toilet paper over the glue. Paste more of the glue on top. Cover the whole pencil, including the cone, then leave it to dry overnight.

Ready to write
Your pencil will now be rock hard and ready to paint with poster or acrylic paint. When it is finished, you'll have a really professional giant Art Attack pencil – and it really writes!

When the paint is dry, go round all the pencil details with a black marker pen.

You can finish off your pencil by writing your name on the side.

Curved edges around the edge of the tip give an authentic pencil look.

Add some foil and paint the end red to make a realistic-looking rubber.

Mix your own wood colour from orange and white paint.

Paint the end of your pencil in a wood colour, then draw in a black lead with a marker pen.

Get a grip!
You'll certainly impress your friends when you sign your name with this enormous pencil. But it's so big that you'll have to get a good grip on it!

THUMBS-UP AWARD

Do you know someone who has recently passed an exam or a test? Why not present them with a thumbs-up award to say "Well done"!

From cardboard to award

Materials

Cardboard and newspaper

Pebble

Sticky tape

Glue mixture

Party cup

Paint

Toilet paper

Scissors

Paintbrush

Marker pen

Remember to stick your thumb out at the side for the thumbs up!

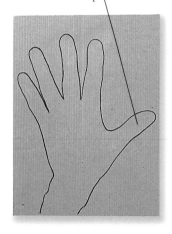

Tape a ball of newspaper to the palm of the hand.

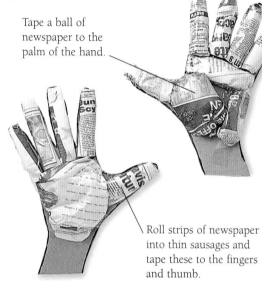

Roll strips of newspaper into thin sausages and tape these to the fingers and thumb.

1 Place your hand on a piece of cardboard and draw round it with a marker pen. Include about 5 cm of the wrist. Cut the hand out.

2 Pad the hand out on both sides with scrunched up newspaper. Then put more tape around the palm and fingers to neaten them up.

3 Bend each of the fingers towards the palm and break in two places, at the base and again half-way up. Hold the fingers in the bent position and tape them in place.

Bend all four fingers towards the palm, but don't bend the thumb.

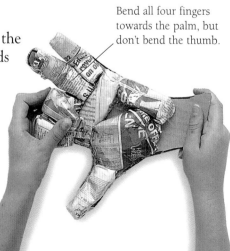

4 Stand the paper cup upside-down on a square of cardboard and tape it in place. Cut or tear the bottom off the cup, then cut a slit in each side of the cup, going a quarter of the way down.

The cup will form the base of your award.

5 Put a large pebble in the cup to add weight to the base. Scrunch up some newspaper and press it into the cup to hold the pebble in place. Slot the wrist of the hand into the slits on the sides of the cup.

6 Tape the hand firmly in place on the cup base. Then cover the whole shape with two layers of toilet paper and glue mixture. Leave it overnight to dry completely.

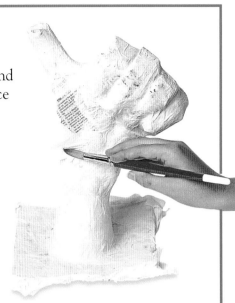

It's a good idea to paint the hand first, in case any paint drips down on to the base.

Gold is a great colour for this award.

Ready to present
Paint your award with poster or acrylic paint. Then it's just a case of presenting it to someone who deserves the thumbs-up award!

Add some brown paint on the palm and between the fingers to give the effect of shading.

Paint the base black.

Mix your own gold
You don't have to buy special gold paint – mix your own gold colour from yellow and orange.

Alternative colour
This award has been painted silver with black shading between the fingers.

JUNK JEWELLERY

Amaze your family and friends by transforming plastic bags, scrap paper, cardboard, and tape into some fun-looking pieces of jewellery.

From bag to bangle

Roll your bag lengthways.

Materials

Wrapping paper

Plastic bag

Bowl of water

Sticky tape

Parcel tape ★

Paint

PVA Glue

Scissors

Paintbrush

1 Take a plastic bag, like those you can get from a supermarket, and roll it up to make a long, thin sausage shape.

Take some gummed parcel tape and soak it in water. Don't worry if you over-soak it.

2 Wind the bag around your hand to make a ring. Then wrap some sticky tape round the ring to secure it.

Use several strips of tape instead of one long one to make it easier to handle.

Glue on small pieces of left-over wrapping paper for decoration.

3 Take some soaked parcel tape and begin winding it tightly around the ring. Cover the whole ring in two or three layers of tape. Then put it aside to dry.

4 Paint the bangle with acrylic paint and decorate it with paper shapes. When dry, cover it with a coat of PVA glue to give it a shiny finish. Leave it to dry again.

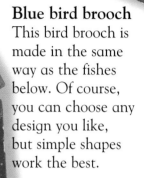

Draw in extra details with a black marker pen.

Brilliant bangles

Your supermarket plastic bag can be magically turned into a fabulous piece of designer jewellery. If you have some waste paper and cardboard, you can create all these other pieces of jewellery too!

Thread your beads on to some colourful string or sewing thread.

Blue bird brooch

This bird brooch is made in the same way as the fishes below. Of course, you can choose any design you like, but simple shapes work the best.

You can decorate your bangles with tissue paper, foil, or even sweet wrappers!

Mix and match necklace

Create beads for this fun necklace by shaping short lengths of soaked gummed tape round one finger. Let the beads dry, then decorate them in the same way as the bangles.

Mix and match different-coloured beads. You can even paint them to match a favourite outfit.

Fishy brooches

These beautiful fish brooches are simple to make. Draw the basic fish shape on to a piece of thick cardboard and cut it out. Next, tape a scrunched-up piece of paper to it. Then follow Steps 3 and 4.

Brooch pins

Turn your designs into brooches by taping a large safety pin to the back of the cardboard base.

CUP MONSTER

Next time you are at a party where everyone has party cups, wait until the end, then clean them out and bring them back to life as a puppet!

From cups to puppet

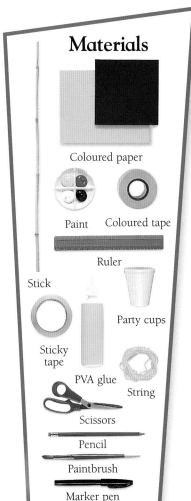

Materials

Coloured paper

Paint   Coloured tape

Ruler

Stick

Party cups

Sticky tape

PVA glue

String

Scissors

Pencil

Paintbrush

Marker pen

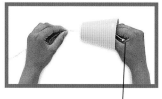

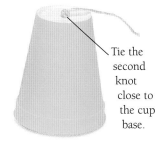

Make sure the first knot ends up inside of the cup.

Tie the second knot close to the cup base.

1 Collect a stack of about 20 clean party cups. Make a hole in the base of each cup by stabbing it with a sharp pencil.

2 Tie a knot at the end of a long piece of string. Thread the string through the hole in the cup, with the knot inside. Then tie a knot on the other side.

Use a marker pen to mark the position of the next knot.

Stick the puppet's eyes here.

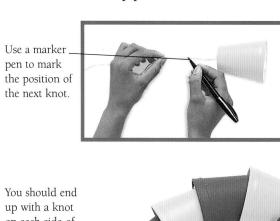

Stick two cups together to make the eyes.

You should end up with a knot on each side of the cup base.

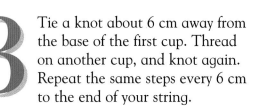

3 Tie a knot about 6 cm away from the base of the first cup. Thread on another cup, and knot again. Repeat the same steps every 6 cm to the end of your string.

4 Take two more cups and glue or staple them together. Put a loop of sticky tape underneath the cups and stick them to the second to last cup on the puppet body.

Scary monster

Don't leave your cup monster puppet bare. Paint it with acrylic paint, or poster paint mixed with PVA glue.

Glue balls of paper inside the eye cups for eyes and add a circle of spiky card eyelashes to complete your cup monster.

Paint some big scary eyes on the eyeballs.

Make your cup monster wriggle and dance by flicking your wrist and twisting the stick.

Paint the cups in alternate colours for a jazzy, stripy look.

You may need to paint the cups more than once to cover them well.

Hanging up the puppet

1 Use some lengths of string to hang up your puppet. Loop one piece through the side of the eyes leaving a length free at both ends.

2 Tie a second piece of string half way along the body to create a curve.

3 You can add some more pieces of string if your puppet is very long. Tie the ends of the string to a stick and secure with tape.

GARBAGE GOBBLER

Is your room cluttered with scraps of paper and other bits of rubbish that you've left strewn all over the floor? Then what you need is a garbage gobbler!

From newspaper to bin

Newspaper

Paint

Toilet paper

Stapler

Sticky tape

Bowl for glue mixture

Scissors

Paintbrush

Marker pen

1 Open two of the newspapers with the centre pages facing up. Tape the pages of each paper together at the top and bottom of the centre creases.

Be careful to keep your fingers out of the stapler.

2 Place one newspaper on top of the other, with the centre pages together. Staple the papers together at the two sides.

You need about three sheets of newspaper to make each eye.

5 Fold the top edge of the bin inwards over the lips and tape it in place all round. To make the eyes, scrunch up two balls of newspaper and tape them to the top edge.

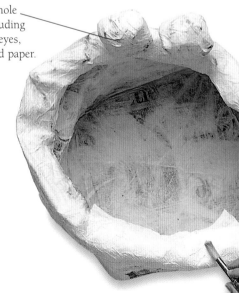

Cover the whole gobbler, including the lips and eyes, with glue and paper.

6 Paint the whole gobbler with the glue mixture. Then lay pieces of kitchen roll on the gobbler and paint more glue mixture over them.

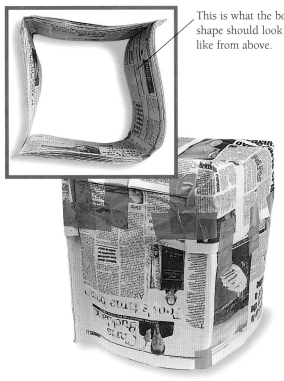

This is what the box shape should look like from above.

Make a sausage by rolling up six sheets of newspaper, and taping them at both ends.

You will need to tape the ends of the long sausage together where they overlap.

3 Open the two papers out and stand them up to form a box shape. Take a third paper and loosely place it over the open top. Fold the edges over the box and tape them in place.

4 For the gobbler lips, make two sausage shapes from newspaper. Overlap an end from each sausage and tape them together. Curl the long sausage into the top edge of the bin.

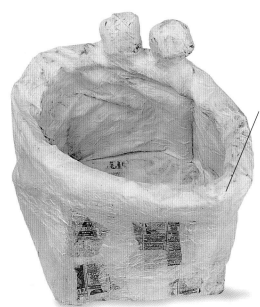

Push this edge down towards the base of the gobbler.

7 While the gobbler is still damp, pull the edge of the lips, opposite the eyes, down towards the base of the gobbler to form the open mouth. Then leave the gobbler to dry.

8 When the gobbler is dry, draw on the features with a marker pen. Outline the edge of the lips and add in details such as the pupils and a highlight on the eyes.

MIGHTY MOUTHS

Here's the finished garbage gobbler. Put it under your desk or, better still, on the other side of your room and see if you can throw your rubbish into its hungry mouth!

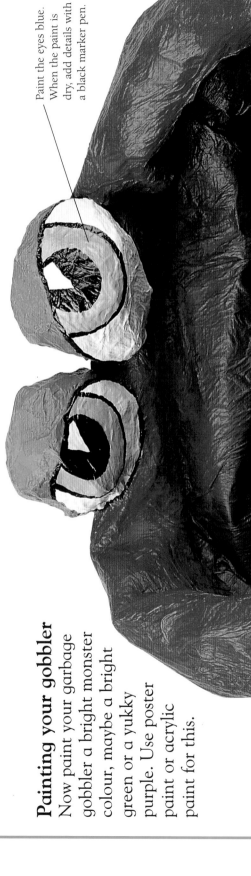

Paint the eyes blue. When the paint is dry, add details with a black marker pen.

Paint the lips and the inside of the mouth bright red.

Painting your gobbler
Now paint your garbage gobbler a bright monster colour, maybe a bright green or a yukky purple. Use poster paint or acrylic paint for this.

Brown shading inside the mouth makes it look even bigger!

Shade the hollows with darker paint to make the skin look more wrinkly.

Paint the gobbler yellow with orange shading between the fingers and toes.

Cut out a cardboard tongue and pad it with some scrunched up newspaper. Tape the tongue to the inside of the mouth.

Outline all the details with a black marker pen.

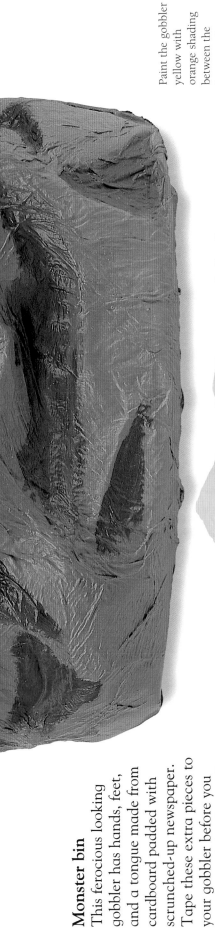

Monster bin

This ferocious looking gobbler has hands, feet, and a tongue made from cardboard padded with scrunched-up newspaper. Tape these extra pieces to your gobbler before you cover it with kitchen roll.

To make the fingers and toes, scrunch up sausage shapes out of newspaper and tape them to the hands and feet.

FOIL PLAQUE

Kitchen foil is a great art material, and you don't need a lot to create a dramatic Art Attack. Try designing one of these foil plaques!

From foil to plaque

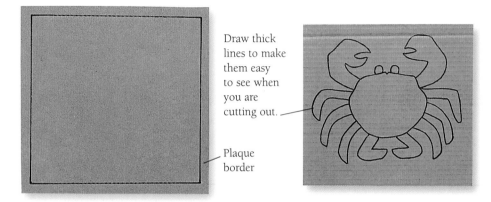

Draw thick lines to make them easy to see when you are cutting out.

Plaque border

Materials

Cardboard

Kitchen foil

PVA glue   Paint   Glue stick

Sticky tape   Toilet paper

Scissors

Ruler

Paintbrush

Marker pen

1 Cut out two pieces of cardboard, roughly 10 cm square. Take one of the pieces and draw a 1 cm border around the edge.

2 Cut out the border in one piece. Then draw a picture on the remaining piece of cardboard, making sure that it fills the whole area.

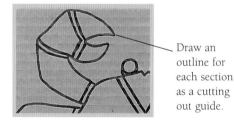

Draw an outline for each section as a cutting out guide.

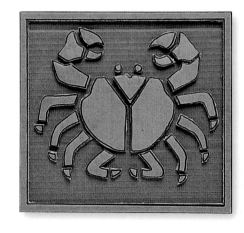

3 Divide your picture into sections, as shown here. Cut out each section carefully, and glue it in position in the centre on the second piece of cardboard.

4 Next, cover one side of your border with some glue and stick it to the front of your plaque. Make sure that the border matches up with the edge of the plaque and fits neatly round the edge of your picture.

5 Next, cover the whole of your picture and frame with PVA glue. Place a piece of kitchen foil over the plaque and gently press it down into all the nooks and crannies with some toilet paper.

6 Water down some poster paint and brush it over the whole picture. Then take a piece of toilet paper and carefully wipe off the wet paint from the raised parts of the picture.

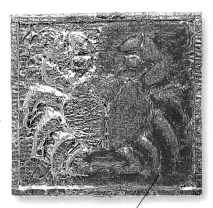

Apply paint to all the nooks and crannies.

Creepy crawly crab

And here it is, your very own kitchen-foil plaque. You could hang this crab plaque in the bathroom along with other pictures on a seaside theme. You could also design a personalized plaque of your initials, or your whole name.

Make the skull features from left-over pieces of cardboard.

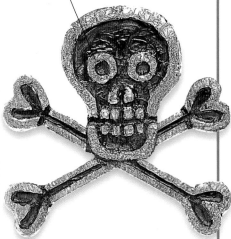

Numbered sections
If you number each section of your picture before you cut them out it will help you reposition them later.

Fold the edges of the kitchen foil over the back of the plaque and tape them down.

The shiny picture stands out on your plaque once the paint is removed.

Skull and crossbones

This scary skull and crossbones plaque is made from several cardboard pieces that are glued together. Paint it dark-blue or purple to give it a creepy look!

CROC POT

What do you do with your wet brush when you are painting? Don't let it drip everywhere – make this crocodile paintbrush holder, instead!

From card to croc

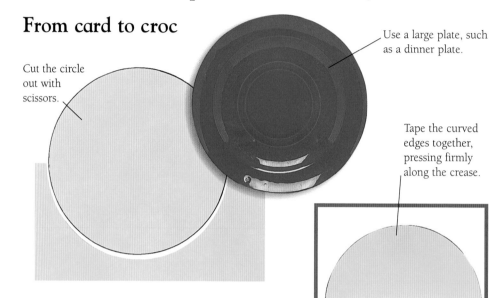

Cut the circle out with scissors.

Use a large plate, such as a dinner plate.

Tape the curved edges together, pressing firmly along the crease.

Materials

Thin card

Newspaper

Plate

Sticky tape

Paint

Toilet paper

Glue mixture

Scissors

Paintbrush

Marker pen

1 Place a plate face down on a piece of thin card or thick paper and draw round it. Then cut out the circle and fold it in half to make a semicircle.

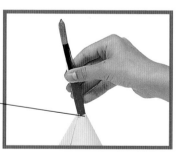

Snip the top off the cone to make a hole to put your paintbrush in.

Scrunch up some newspaper into balls to make the eyes and nose.

2 Bend the straight edge of the semicircle round to make a cone shape. Overlap the two halves of the straight edge by about 6-7 cm and use a strip of tape to hold the cone together.

3 Make the eyes and nose from newspaper. Tape two newspaper balls at the base of the cone to make the eyes and two smaller balls near the point to form the nostrils.

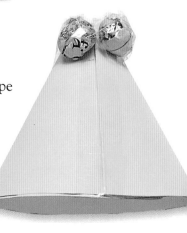

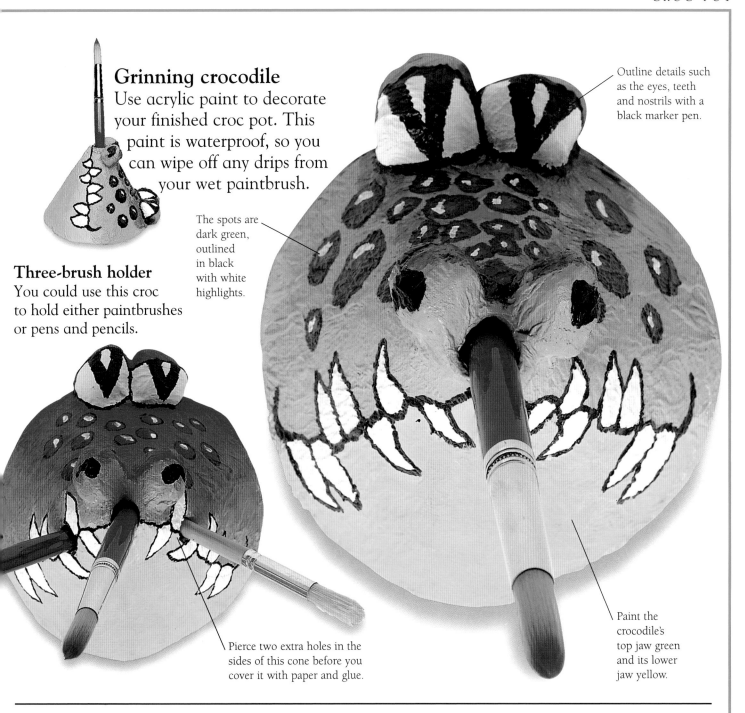

Grinning crocodile
Use acrylic paint to decorate your finished croc pot. This paint is waterproof, so you can wipe off any drips from your wet paintbrush.

Outline details such as the eyes, teeth and nostrils with a black marker pen.

Three-brush holder
You could use this croc to hold either paintbrushes or pens and pencils.

The spots are dark green, outlined in black with white highlights.

Pierce two extra holes in the sides of this cone before you cover it with paper and glue.

Paint the crocodile's top jaw green and its lower jaw yellow.

4 Paste the glue mixture on to the cone. Lay strips of toilet paper over it and then add another layer of the glue mixture. Cover the head, inside and out, including the eyes and nostrils.

Be careful not to cover the paintbrush hole.

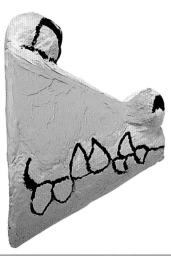

5 Leave the head to dry overnight. Then, draw in eyes, mouth, teeth, and nostrils with a black marker pen. Finally, paint your crocodile in bright colours, complete with big white teeth.

ROCKET TIDY

Are you always losing your pencils? Do you wish you could find your pens when you need them? Then look no further – this rocket pen tidy is for you!

Materials

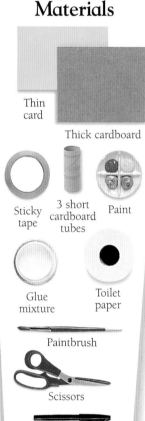

Thin card

Thick cardboard

Sticky tape

3 short cardboard tubes

Paint

Glue mixture

Toilet paper

Paintbrush

Scissors

Marker pen

From cardboard tube to rocket

Roll the cone tightly, starting from a corner.

Remove the uncut tube from inside.

1 Cut lengthways down two cardboard tubes. Wrap one of these slit tubes around the third uncut tube. Cover the gap with a piece of thin card and tape in place.

2 Roll the other split tube back on itself to make a cone. Tape the cone together, snip off the excess cardboard at the base, and tape to the top of the outer tube.

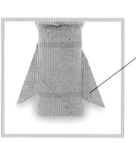

Cut out triangles from leftover cardboard and tape to the bottom of the rocket for wings.

3 Add cardboard wings to complete your rocket. Next, coat the rocket in glue mixture and cover it with strips of toilet paper until the rocket is totally covered. Leave it to dry overnight.

4 Now you are ready to decorate your rocket. First draw in some details with a marker pen. You could also add some portholes, and some rivets and screws. Then paint your rocket and leave it on one side to dry.

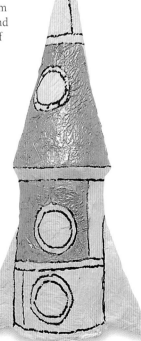

5

To make the rocket base, take the uncut cardboard tube and glue firmly on to a square of thick cardboard and then leave it to dry.

Draw a zig-zag explosion around the base of the tube.

6

When the glue has dried, carefully cut along the zig-zag line and stand the tube upright. Next paint both the base and the tube in bright, fiery colours.

Space rockets

Once you have made a rocket pen tidy for yourself, why not make some more for the rest of the family. Then no-one will ever be without a pencil again!

You can use silver-coloured paint to give the rocket a metallic finish.

Hidden details

Remember to go over your marker-pen details once the paint has dried to make them really stand out.

Blast off!

Now collect together your pens and pencils and pop them into your rocket base. Slip the rocket lid over the top and you're ready for blast off!

Make your base fairly wide so that it won't topple over with the weight of the pens.

Mix red and yellow paint together for a really explosive look.

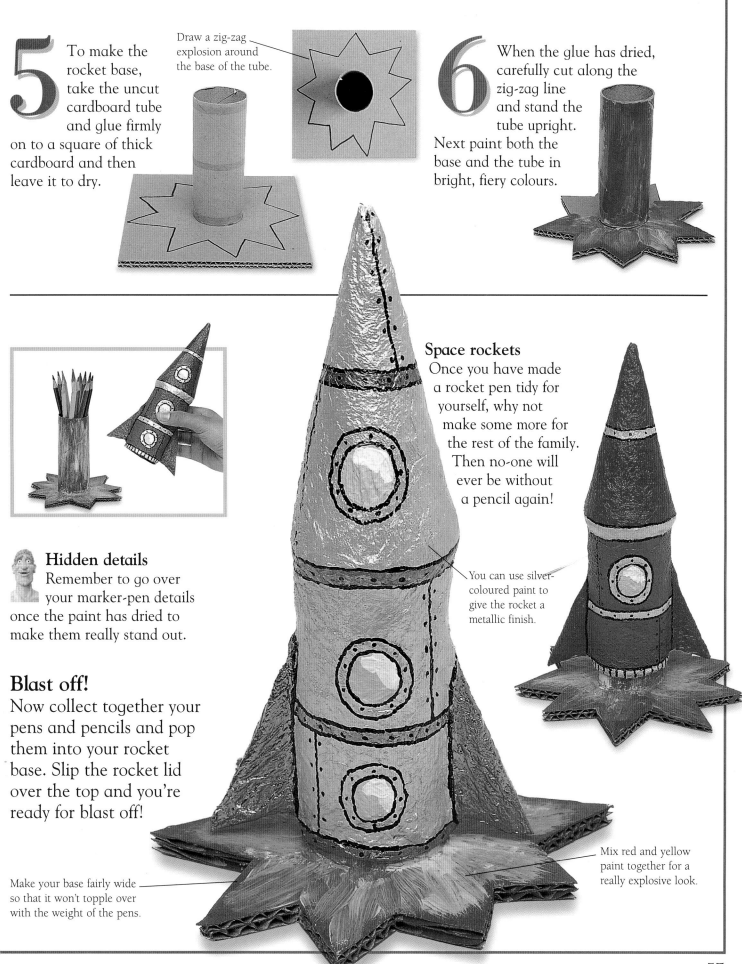

BOOK BUDDY

Do you suffer from toppling books in your bedroom? What you need is one of these heavy-weight bookends!

From sugar bag to bookend

The legs need to be chunky to stop the figure falling flat on its face.

Materials

PVA glue Newspaper

Gravel

Toilet paper

Paint

Tape

Glue mixture

Sugar bag

Scissors

Paintbrush

Marker pen

1 Take an empty sugar or flour bag and almost fill it with gravel or small stones to weight it down. Fold the top of the bag over and tape it.

2 Scrunch up some small pieces of newspaper to make two L-shaped legs. Tape them firmly to the base of the bag.

Make the nose from a small ball of toilet paper.

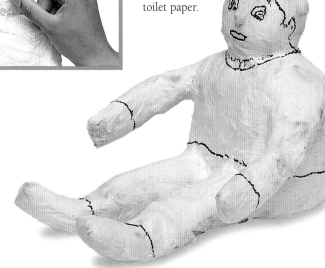

5 Wrap strips of toilet paper around the figure then use a paintbrush to cover your figure with glue mixture. Cover the whole body with two layers of paper and glue mixture, then leave it to dry overnight.

6 Once the figure is dry, it is ready to paint. Before you add any colour, use a marker pen to draw on some facial features, hair, and to mark the outline of the figure's clothes.

Bend the arms
in the middle
and at the ends
to make elbows
and hands.

Stick the legs out
in front of the bag.

Make the head
about the same
size as your fist.

3 Build up the rest of the body with
scrunched-up pieces of newspaper.
Make two long sausage shapes for
arms and tape them securely to the
top of the bag, on either side.

4 Next, take some pieces of newspaper
and scrunch them up into a ball.
Wrap tape around the ball to hold
it together, then tape it securely to
the top of the bag to make the head.

A marker pen is ideal for
drawing in very small
details on the face.

Draw black
lines on the
hair for a more
realistic effect.

7 Now paint your figure in bright colours.
Remember to paint all the way around
your figure, including the back of the
clothes, and the hair. Paint the hands in
skin tones and paint shoes on the feet.

8 Leave the figure to dry overnight.
Then add in extra details with a
marker pen. When the figure is
ready, coat it in a layer of PVA
glue for a shiny finish.

SHELF BUDDIES

There's no limit to the book buddies you can make. Try your hand at a dancer or footballer, or make one that looks like you!

This figure has a cartoon face, with big round eyes and a button nose.

Johnnie jumper

Now you have finished your book buddy all you need to do is choose which shelf you will put it on! Wherever you choose to put it, your bookend will be a useful addition to your room.

Heavy weights

You don't have to use your book buddy to prop up books. A small one will make an ideal paper weight, while a large heavy one could be used to prop open a door.

Seeing double

Use your bookends to prop up books on your shelves or on the floor. If you have lots of books, why not put a buddy at each end of your row of books?

This figure is wearing trainers. Complete the look by adding tread patterns on the shoe soles.

60

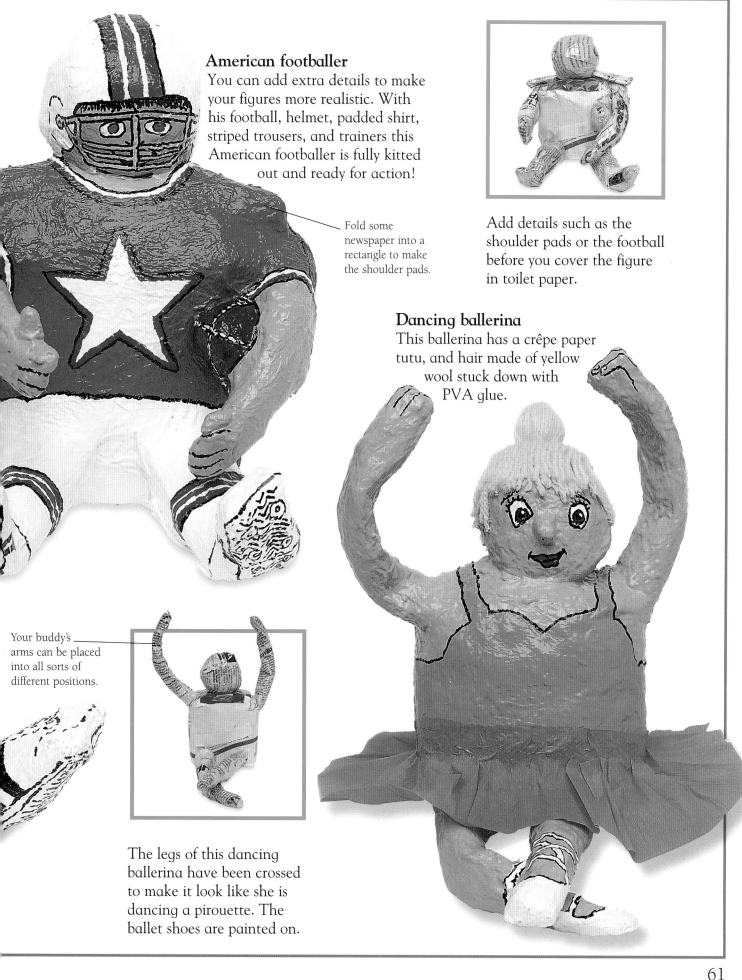

American footballer

You can add extra details to make your figures more realistic. With his football, helmet, padded shirt, striped trousers, and trainers this American footballer is fully kitted out and ready for action!

Fold some newspaper into a rectangle to make the shoulder pads.

Add details such as the shoulder pads or the football before you cover the figure in toilet paper.

Dancing ballerina

This ballerina has a crêpe paper tutu, and hair made of yellow wool stuck down with PVA glue.

Your buddy's arms can be placed into all sorts of different positions.

The legs of this dancing ballerina have been crossed to make it look like she is dancing a pirouette. The ballet shoes are painted on.

HANDY TIPS

These pages contain lots of top tips and helpful hints from Art Attack that will help you make the projects in this book.

Drawing on dark card
When drawing on dark card, use a light-coloured pen or pencil so your markings are easier to see.

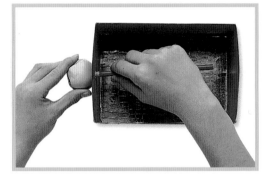

Making a hole in card
Place some modelling clay under the card. Press a sharp pencil through the card into the clay to make a neat hole.

Removing papier mâché moulds
Papier mâché moulds are easier to remove if covered in cling wrap first.

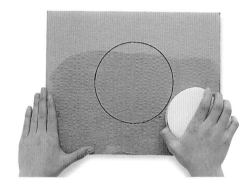

Cutting cardboard
Thick cardboard is easier to cut if you first wet it slightly with water.

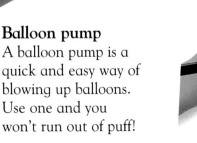

Balloon pump
A balloon pump is a quick and easy way of blowing up balloons. Use one and you won't run out of puff!

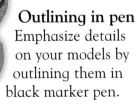

Outlining in pen
Emphasize details on your models by outlining them in black marker pen.

Using PVA glue

PVA glue

Poster paint

Making acrylic paint
Make your own waterproof paint by mixing poster paint with PVA glue.

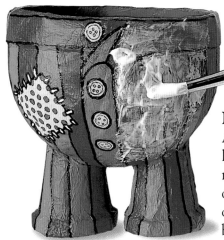

Painting with PVA glue
A coat of PVA glue gives a lovely, shiny finish to your models. When you brush it on it will look white, but once it has dried it will become shiny and clear.

Painting tips

Orange

Red

Yellow

Mixing paint colours
Create different colours and shades by mixing your paints together.

Applying paint
Create interesting paint effects by applying paint with paper or a cloth.

Hanging a frame

Secure a loop of string with tape.

Tape the ring tab to the top of your frame.

The stand is a long, thin triangle with the tip cut off.

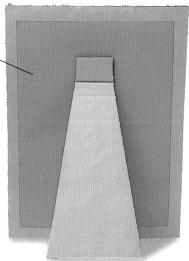

Hanging heavy frames
Place tape through a metal ring and stick the ends together. Tape the tab to the frame back.

Hanging light frames
Use a loop of string and tape to hang lightweight frames, such as the shrunken head.

Free-standing frame
Cut out a cardboard stand, as shown. Bend the top part over and glue it to the frame back.

INDEX